With All My
heart

(RE)GROUP, (RE)THINK, OR (RE)POSITION
YOURSELF DURING TOUGH TIMES

Nikole Holt

Quantity sales. Special discounts are available on quantity purchases. For details, please contact the publisher at brightbeautiesltd@gmail.com.

Cover Design: Andrea Huff

Interior Book Design: S.J. Forester

ISBN-13: 978-0-578-57452-3

With All My Heart

(Re)group, (Re)think, or (Re)position
Yourself During Tough Times

Dedication

Dedicated to my mother, Ruth E. Thomas. She was a beautiful warrior that fought hate with love, injustice with righteousness and loneliness with friendship. Her greatest fight was for her family, for she truly loved us with all her heart!

And to my husband, Milton Holt Sr., through everything we have experienced, I could not imagine doing life without you.

Introduction

Who do you love with all your heart? Your mother, father, brother, sister, child(ren), grandmother, grandfather, uncle, aunt, maybe a really close friend, or all of the above? Is there anything you would not do for that loved one? And when you think of love, does it invoke joy or sadness?

Love can be expressed numerous ways. It can be as simple as saying 'I love you,' or as grand as elaborate gifts. It can be expressed by a gentle smile or by donating an organ. Love is both big and small, majestic and modest, work and relaxation. Yet whether it is expressed in any of these modes it is still love.

It has been almost two years, as I begin writing, since my beloved mother passed away, and to say the least, it has been a heart-wrenching journey accepting that I would not physically talk with her on a daily basis. My emotions walk a tight-rope between the memories of love and the realization of her absence. My thoughts of her can take me from laughter to crying within seconds. The only way I have survived this jagged terrain of grief is my relationship with Jesus Christ! God has been my comforter, my healer, my provider, and my friend. Yet I have unwittingly kept a distance.

The purpose of this devotional is to provide a gentle reminder of what it means to seek God with all our heart and find His loving arms waiting for you. No matter what circumstance we find ourselves in life, God is always (and I do mean always) with us, every step of the way. Whether we attempt to shut Him out or welcome Him in, God is there with us. I continue to learn that I can trust God again and again, no matter what happens along my life's journey.

As we begin this journey of re-establishing our footing from a tragic loss, a broken heart, a devastating disappointment, or the many difficult situations we face in life, I hope you will remember to always trust in God in all things. This prefix 're', meaning 'again' or 'again and again', to indicate repetition, has fueled me to truly keep moving after my mom's death. I had to remind myself again and again not to be angry with the world (or with God), that God's unwavering love was enough to carry me through the emptiness I felt. And I could hear her telling me, "Nikki, you have my grandchildren to take care of!" so just staying numb was not an option.

My prayer is that after 21 days you will notice the ground you stand on is a bit more stable. You will be able to walk, leap, or even run with the horses. But most of all, you will be able to encourage someone else to be that brave warrior of God's design.

After each day, there is a page where you can write out your own thoughts and/or prayer that corresponds with that word. Don't be afraid to tear out the "Thoughts and Prayer" page and stick it on your mirror, dashboard, or wherever you can see it on a regular basis, so that your spirit is opened to know God's love.

Day 1

RECALIBRATE

:to change the way you do or think about something (dictionary.cambridge.org/us/, 2019)

I waited patiently for the Lord; And He inclined to me, And heard my cry. He also brought me up out of a horrible pit, Out of the miry clay, And set my feet upon a rock, And established my steps.

(PSALMS 40:1-2, NKJV)

There are moments in life that hit so hard that you lose your footing. It is in these times where your thoughts struggle to recover some sort of stability. It is difficult to wait patiently when you can't seem to catch your breath because of the hurt. Psalm 40 tells us "And He inclined to me." The Lord will move in close to hear your cry. As you put your trust in Jesus, He will bring you up from your dark place and clean the muck of the pit from your feet. This is important since your feet represent movement. God has a particular function for you, so you have to keep living. The Lord will recalibrate the circumstances of your life to steady you and bring Him glory. He will do it by putting you on a solid foundation and directing your next steps.

The death of my mom was a deep cut in my spirit. It was devastating. Although her passing was almost two months to the day of the initial incident, I still was not ready to lose her. And she shared with me that she was not ready to die. That was really tough. I did not know how to reconcile those emotions, because it was hard to accept that God had allowed it to happen. But I felt God with me even with my mixed emotions concerning the situation. There is always something, I like to call it a nugget, to keep me from depression. Because he heard my cry, these nuggets helped me to make the needed adjustments in my mood so I could function at my fullest. I needed to be of a sound mind during those two months. And God would do it again and again for me.

Prayer: Lord, I am thankful that You hear the depth of my sorrow and You do not leave me in that darkness. Thank You for making adjustments to my journey that keep my feet steady and my steps guided by Your intentions. For in You, Lord, I place my trust. Amen.

Day 1

RE-CALIBRATE:
THOUGHTS AND PRAYER

_____

_____

_____

_____

_____

_____

_____

_____

_____

_____

_____

_____

_____

_____

_____

_____

_____

_____

_____

_____

_____

_____

_____

_____

_____

_____

Day 2

REALIGN

:to put something into a new or correct position.
(dictionary.cambridge.org/us/, 2019)

Restore to me the joy of Your salvation, And uphold me by Your generous Spirit.

(PSALMS 51:12, NKJV)

Some life events can provoke expressions of grief, depression, worry, or anxiety that can affect your mind, body, and spirit in ways that you were not prepared to handle. In these moments of calamity, you will need to place your burdens and emotions in the hands of our Savior. Jesus can restore us in a manner that will either place us in a positive state of mind or center us to that former place of stability which helps us to regain our footing. He will open our hearts to receive a joy that the events of this life cannot quench. Our life journey may have moments that can be so tough that you question your ability to survive. I want you to remember to keep moving forward, realizing that with each step, He is holding (and yes, sometimes carrying) you by His generous (substantial, lavish, large, liberal, princely) Spirit.

For the past year I have experienced anxiety in ways that I never expected. It has made me question my abilities and intelligence. I have been so out of whack that it has taken a series of events (which God orchestrated) to bring me back into purposeful alignment. God has reminded me that in Him my steps are ordered. Therefore, even when things do not go as I expect them to, and it gets me off balance, He is there to hold me up.

Prayer: Lord, I am grateful that I do not have to carry the responsibility of keeping myself all together. I can rest in Your ability to restore the joy in me when life throws me around like a rag doll or mentally tries to take me out. Help me to remember that it is through Your sacrifice and redemption I receive an everlasting joy.

Day 2

REALIGN: THOUGHTS AND PRAYER

_____
_____
_____
_____
_____
_____
_____
_____
_____
_____
_____
_____
_____
_____
_____
_____
_____
_____
_____
_____
_____
_____
_____
_____

Day 3

RE-ADAPT

Adapt: to adjust to different conditions or
uses, or to change to meet different situations
(dictionary.cambridge.org/us/, 2019)

*And he prayed again, and the heaven gave rain, and the
earth produced its fruit.*

(JAMES 5:18, NKJV)

After experiencing a tragic event in your life, there is a process you will undoubtedly go through with your emotions. It may be anger, bitterness, sadness, or guilt to name a few. You play it out in your head over and over wondering if you could have done something different to prevent what happened, or at least soften the blow. This only wreaks havoc on your emotional wellbeing. A change in how you think, move, and are is happening in your life. Remember to keep praying. Although life is now different, in order to move beyond this heartbreaking event, you will need to surrender your emotions to God so that He can grow fruit from a dry place.

After my mom's initial surgery, I had hoped that she would recover. Then she had to have another surgery, and things started to go down from there. Yet I still had hope she would come home. Yes, things would change since she would need assistance, and my dad would not be able to do it on his own, but I still had hope. So when she died (although God did give me two months to accept the inevitable), it still was a devastating event. I could not sit there and watch my mom take her last breath. And I still wish I could have been stronger just to hold her hand.

You need to know that things have or will change after dealing with a difficult event in your life. But you also need to know that God will see you through, and you will laugh again and have joy again. May your fruit be sweeter because of your pain and ultimately be an encouragement to others to continue the journey.

Prayer: Lord, thank You for always covering me in any season I find myself in life. Even through a day, or days, of torrential rain, may I remember that You are always with me. Let me not forget that rain brings a cleansing and fosters growth in my natural habitat. You will produce fruit along my journey as I grow through the changing conditions of my life.

Day 3

Readapt: Thoughts and Prayer

_____
_____
_____
_____
_____
_____
_____
_____
_____
_____
_____
_____
_____
_____
_____
_____
_____
_____
_____
_____
_____
_____
_____
_____
_____

Day 4

REMORSE

:a strong feeling of guilt and regret about something you have done (dictionary.cambridge.org/us/, 2019)

A brother offended is harder to win than a strong city,
And contentions are like the bars of a castle.

(PROVERBS 18:19, NKJV)

Whether it is happens in a moment of selfishness, anger, retaliation, or down-right on purpose, when we are the offender and have caused the hurt, at some point the Holy Spirit within will draw us to a place of remorse. Take that moment to realize how your actions can hinder the progress of the person you have hurt. As the offender, resist the need to justify your actions. If you are unwilling to ask for forgiveness it only strengthens the walls of isolation and weakens your ability to be used as a good instrument for the Kingdom of God.

As I noted in Day 3, I was not mentally capable of sitting by my mom's bedside waiting for her to take her last breath. Everything in me wanted to do it but my mind was over-riding that desire. I would have probably (no, surely) gone into a state of depression. But I felt like I let my mom down by not being by her side until the very end which was a deep regret for me. I could allow my thoughts to keep me bound and in a perpetual state of guilt. This guilt could affect my relationship with my family or how I live going forward. I had to release those feelings and simply let her know I was sorry for not being there at that moment. God settled in my spirit that I was a great daughter to my mom and reminded me how she loved me so. And that is enough for me.

Prayer: Lord, I thank You for allowing tough life experiences to keep me humble in spirit and not bitter. I understand that remorse is not to send me into a dark pit but to take a good look at my actions, seek forgiveness or healing, and move forward. As my sister or brother's keeper, I wish to unite not divide relationships. Therefore, when I have feelings of deep regret, may it lead me to repentance and a new level of growth.

Day 4

REMORSE: THOUGHTS AND PRAYER

_____
_____
_____
_____
_____
_____
_____
_____
_____
_____
_____
_____
_____
_____
_____
_____
_____
_____
_____
_____
_____
_____
_____
_____
_____
_____
_____
_____

Day 5

REAFFIRM

:to state something as true again, or to state your support for something again (dictionary. cambridge.org/us/, 2019)

Why are you cast down, O my soul? And why are you disquieted within me? Hope in God, for I shall yet praise Him For the help of His countenance.

(PSALMS 42:5, NKJV)

When you are in the eye of a storm, remember to take just a moment to praise God (a moment is all you need to make that connection). The New Living Translation of Psalm 45:5 states it this way: "Why am I discouraged? Why is my heart so sad? I will put my hope in God! I will praise him again - my Savior." This same scripture is noted two additional times, Psalm 42:11 and 43:5, which indicates a need to be reminded. It can be so dark when you are facing difficulty. So you must take that split-second to reaffirm your hope in whom Jesus is in your life and not the current difficult event. Praise in that moment may not be a shout or dance or listening to uplifting music. It may be a modest smile or a "thank you, Lord" or simply closing your eyes and knowing He has you. Taking that moment to remember His sovereignty over your sadness will help carry you to another day.

Have you ever had an experience where someone makes you question your worthiness? Or maybe your faith was being questioned? Or maybe your loyalty? In these moments, the stress levels or anxiety can be off the chart. I have experienced all of this in my professional career, and it nearly took me out. My conversations were like, "Really God?", "God what is going on? Why have you not opened a door yet and released me from this nightmare?" Oh, it was bad. I had moments where I literally cried because I just could not believe what I was going through and God had not moved on my behalf yet. Don't get so caught up in the hardship that you overlook how God has kept you and the expectation of your deliverance. Keep your hope in God; that he is working all things out for your good. Is this tough to do? Of course it is hard! May that small voice reaffirm that you are stronger than you think and give you fresh hope to wait on God.

Prayer: Lord, thank You for reminding me to look to You when life has dealt me a blow. Reminding me not to dwell in that place of darkness and that all I need is that flicker of light to know You are with me. When I feel like giving up, I will reiterate my hope is in Jesus!

Day 5

Reaffirm: Thoughts and Prayer

_____
_____
_____
_____
_____
_____
_____
_____
_____
_____
_____
_____
_____
_____
_____
_____
_____
_____
_____
_____
_____
_____
_____
_____
_____
_____

Day 6

RE-AWAKEN

:to become or make aware of (something) again
(www.thefreedictionary.com, 2019)

"Then He who sat on the throne said, "Behold, I make all things new." And He said to me, "Write, for these words are true and faithful."

(REVELATION 21:5, NKJV)

Have you ever broken something and thought, "This can never be fixed!" Then you decide to take it to an expert. After you have entrusted them to repair your item, it is returned to you like it was never broken. When you give your brokenness to the Master, our Sovereign God, He begins to repair you from the inside out. When you cast your burdens on the Lord, He will keep you through everything that comes your way. It does not mean life will be without issues, problems, or difficulty. However, life will still be meaningful as you go through your tough seasons. I challenge you to be conscience of the in-between moments during your privation to see the sun shining on you.

Writing this devotional has stirred the creativity that has been dimmed for quite a while. It is taking me out of my comfort zone. It is pushing me to trust God on new heights while dealing with difficulty. God has awakened dream buds and I'm excited to see what Jesus does with them. I'm also scared to be stretched outside of my normal acceptable level of risk. Since my mom's death, I did not realize that I have been in a perpetual daze that was not pointed in a forward direction. It has been work, family, sleep, and repeat. It feels refreshing to see my desire to be creative reawaken.

Prayer: Lord, I thank You for the breakthrough moments along my journey that allows Your loving kindness to emerge in my darkness and strengthen my faith. Any tough events in my life can never overtake the light You shine upon me. Make things new, Lord.

Day 6

Reawaken: Thoughts and Prayer

_____

_____

_____

_____

_____

_____

_____

_____

_____

_____

_____

_____

_____

_____

_____

_____

_____

_____

_____

_____

_____

_____

_____

_____

_____

_____

_____

Day 7

REMINISCE

:to talk or write about past experiences that you remember with pleasure (dictionary.cambridge.org/us/, 2019)

When my soul fainted within me, I remembered the Lord; And my prayer went up to You, Into Your holy temple.

(JONAH 2:7, NKJV)

Why does the Lord give us the ability to reminisce on past events? I believe it is to help us recall the blissful moments of life. When we are deeply hurt, it seems easy to relive the heartache over and over again and difficult to remember the good things in our life. Reminiscing allows us to measure how far we have come, and it provides hope in our journey ahead. Even if you have to think real hard on the wonderful events that have happened to you thus far, it is well worth the boost for your inner spirit. When you are at your weakness point, remember that the Lord is ALWAYS with you and do not forget to pray.

I remember when I had a conversation with my mother about the times she would tell me that I could not go to the skating rink or to hang with my friends this time because I needed to stay home. She began to tell me that she had to say "no" to me sometimes in order to remind me that I was not raising myself.

Of course, I did not understand this reasoning back then. Especially when I knew I was doing well in school. But looking back, I realize she had to give me boundaries and help me understand that she always had my best interests at the heart of her decisions regarding me. Now, I'm teaching my children about boundaries. Having the ability to ponder on my past has given me the opportunity to think about how much I have grown: as a wife, mother, daughter, and friend. It helps me to embrace the adventures that are coming (God willing) and know that even when the ride is a bit bumpy it is still worth experiencing.

Prayer: Lord, when my heart faints in difficult moments, I am grateful that I can rest in Your care because Your goodness is indescribable. I remember when You gave me laughter in the midst of my tears. I remember the wins among the losses. I remember the victories over the defeats. Thank You for allowing me to remember my good and bad experiences and giving me hope to journey onward.

Day 7

Reminisce: Thoughts and Prayer

_____
_____
_____
_____
_____
_____
_____
_____
_____
_____
_____
_____
_____
_____
_____
_____
_____
_____
_____
_____
_____
_____
_____
_____
_____

Day 8

RELINQUISH

:to give up something, such as a responsibility or claim (dictionary.cambridge.org/us/, 2019)

Commit your way to the Lord, Trust also in Him, And He shall bring it to pass.

(PSALM 37:5, NKJV)

When my mom passed away, I felt like I was dealt a bad hand. You could not tell me that my mom would go home to glory the way she did. It was tough. I could feel the grief taking me into a dark pit. I had to relinquish the desire to be angry and to settle into that pit. I had to consciously commit to healing, trust God with my heart, and know that Jesus will bring me to a point of emotional reconciliation so that I could be released from a regretful mourning to a healthy mourning where healing could take its rightful place in the process.

What part of relinquishing is difficult for you? Is it the commitment, trusting, or waiting for that thing to manifest within your life? There are times when I make the commitment yet struggle with trusting God and waiting for Him bring it forth. Then, there are those moments where I completely trust God, yet I have made no real commitment, let alone enduring the process to get to manifestation. But oh, when I do finally surrender my need to control and decide to commit my ways to the Lord **and** place my trust in Him, He gives me the strength to wait for it. Remember, when you think you do not have the capacity to endure any more weight, surrender the burden to your Heavenly Father who loves you. God will see you through it.

Prayer: Thank You Jesus for Your patience with me. I know I can be stubborn when I want what I want. Yet, You lovingly correct me and wait for me to abandon the need to do it my way. I am totally committed to You and whole-heartedly trust in You as I seek Your direction to walk in the plan You have for my life.

Day 8

RELINQUISH: THOUGHTS AND PRAYER

_____
_____
_____
_____
_____
_____
_____
_____
_____
_____
_____
_____
_____
_____
_____
_____
_____
_____
_____
_____
_____
_____
_____
_____
_____

Day 9

REMASTER

:to make a new master (a recording from which all copies are made) of an earlier recording, usually in order to produce copies with better sound quality (dictionary.cambridge.org/us/, 2019)

The Lord gave another message to Jeremiah. He said, "Go down to the potter's shop, and I will speak to you there." So I did as he told me and found the potter working at his wheel. But the jar he was making did not turn out as he had hoped, so he crushed it into a lump of clay again and started over. Then the Lord gave me this message: "O Israel, can I not do to you as this potter has done to his clay? As the clay is in the potter's hand, so are you in my hand.

(JEREMIAH 18:1-6, NLT)

How many times have you made a dish, worked on a project, or planned an event/outing that did not turn out the way you envisioned it? Trying to maneuver a "redo" of the situation can be frustrating when things do not turn out as planned. It may even push you to respond in a negative manner.

When these moments arise, I want to be placed on the potter's wheel, seeking God to show me the best way to respond. I do not always hit the target that will make God smile. However, I'm thankful for His grace and mercy, and I know the Master Potter is not finished with His craftsmanship. Although the shaping and molding of our character can be very uncomfortable (and some-times take us to the edge of our sanity), God always does this task with love and purpose.

My mom used to say, "Nikki, why do you have to touch the fire to see that it is hot." There have been times when the decisions I have made were not the best. I have made them out of desperation, anger, or simply thinking that I know. Yet God has never used my bad decisions solely for chastisement but to make me better, wiser. I am thankful that God sharpens my image to look more like Him.

Prayer: Thank You Lord for always being with me. Even when what I'm going through can make it seem that You are miles away. I realize at those very moments, Jesus has placed me on His potter's wheel; reshaping me to trust Him more, love Him more, and rely on Him more. I'm grateful that You do not leave me with a dull outlook on life or dull hearing. You have always used everything to enhance my quality of life and ability to love, in spite of how I feel.

REMASTER: THOUGHTS AND PRAYER

_____
_____
_____
_____
_____
_____
_____
_____
_____
_____
_____
_____
_____
_____
_____
_____
_____
_____
_____
_____
_____
_____
_____
_____
_____
_____

Day 10

RESURGE

:to rise again, as from desuetude or from virtual extinction (www.dictionary.com, 2019)

"And go quickly and tell His disciples that He is risen from the dead, and indeed He is going before you into Galilee; there you will see Him. Behold, I have told you."
(MATTHEW 28:7, NKJV)

I spent one year in college after I graduated from high school. When I came home for summer break, I was fortunate enough to get a government summer job. Well, I made the decision not to go back to college and just work. My parents were very disappointed with my decision, and my mom declared that when I did go back to school I would have to pay for it on my own. Initially, I took a few classes at the local community college and then moved to the local university but stopped because it was just too much. I basically gave up. However, after almost eleven years, I made the decision to go for it again. But this time was different. I had the strength and determination that was not there before. Within the next 10 years, I completed my undergrad and master's degree (and was blessed that my parents were able to celebrate both events with me).

Jesus went to the cross and died for our sins. Then He did what no one else could do, he was resurrected. What is God trying to resurge in your life? Maybe a forgotten dream, a severed relationship, or a hopeful heart? Whatever it may be, know that Jesus has the power to resuscitate any forgotten dream or seemingly dead situation for His glory.

Prayer: Even when I have given up on myself, You never do Lord. Thank You again and again.

Day 10

RESURGE: THOUGHTS AND PRAYER

_____
_____
_____
_____
_____
_____
_____
_____
_____
_____
_____
_____
_____
_____
_____
_____
_____
_____
_____
_____
_____
_____
_____
_____
_____

Day 11

RELENTLESS

:continuing in a determined way without any interruption (dictionary.cambridge.org/us/, 2019)

Ask, and it will be given to you; seek, and you will find; knock, and it will be opened to you. For everyone who asks receives, and he who seeks finds, and to him who knocks it will be opened.

(MATTHEW 7:7-8, NKJV)

As I mentioned in Day 10, it took me a long time to complete my undergrad degree once I really got serious about it. There were many days that I wondered if this was for me and many nights that I literally cried sitting in front of the computer trying to finish an assignment or project or respond to a group discussion. I was a wife, worked full time, and had three young children. I had many talks with God about the whole process. Yet no matter the emotional rollercoaster I found myself on, God helped me to be persistent to achieve my goal.

The process of asking, seeking, and knocking should not be taken lightly. They all represent some sort of an action on your part. Realize that to ask is to be in a dialogue with someone else because you are requesting information and you expect a response. To seek is a deeper level attempt to find something out. And to knock is to make your presence known.

In order for you to fully utilize the gifts and talents that God has bestowed upon you, you have to relentlessly pursue His will.

Ask God daily, "What is on the agenda for today?" Seek God's will, and your steps will be guided as you read the Bible and mature in your personal relationship with Him. And finally, don't be afraid to make your love for God known as He open doors for you along the journey.

> *Prayer: Lord, thank You for being persistent in shaping me to be a reflection of love in today's society. Because of Your love towards me, I am able to have a daily conversation with You, to get direction from You as You reveal Your will. When I do this, I will see You increase my territory for Your glory.*

Day 11

Relentless: Thoughts and Prayer

_____
_____
_____
_____
_____
_____
_____
_____
_____
_____
_____
_____
_____
_____
_____
_____
_____
_____
_____
_____
_____
_____
_____

Day 12

REFINE

:to make a substance pure by removing unwanted material (dictionary.cambridge.org/us/, 2019)

Behold, I have refined you, but not as silver; I have tested you in the furnace of affliction.

(ISAIAH 48:10, NKJV)

In the natural, the refining process for silver is done by holding it over the hottest part of the fire in order to burn away the impurities. As God molds us into His image, there is a process of stripping away elements of our character that do not reflect the heart of God. The goal is to be more like Jesus: loving, forgiving, giver, and empathetic to name a few characteristics.

Marriage has been my refiner process. It has taken me to places where I thought recovery was almost impossible. Yet God has used it as an instrument to teach me how to forgive, what unconditional love looks like, and to think more of my spouse than myself (even when I felt wronged). Do you know how tough this can be when you feel like the other person owes you an apology for the offense? The impurities, such as bitterness, anger, jealousy, and retaliation, are burned away as I remember my marriage covenant we made before God, family, and friends.

Prayer: Thank You Lord for not leaving me in an impure state of being. You continue to improve my character by pruning dead leaves that could stunt or even stop my growth. Lord, I will always look to You to create in me a clean heart as You mold my character.

Day 12

REFINE: THOUGHTS AND PRAYER

_____
_____
_____
_____
_____
_____
_____
_____
_____
_____
_____
_____
_____
_____
_____
_____
_____
_____
_____
_____
_____
_____
_____

Day 13

REFOCUS

:to put more effort into particular activities, in the belief that you will make a company more successful (dictionary.cambridge.org/us/, 2019)

"Finally, brethren, whatever things are true, whatever things are noble, whatever things are just, whatever things are pure, whatever things are lovely, whatever things are of good report, if there is any virtue and if there is anything praiseworthy—meditate on these things."

(PHILIPPIANS 4:8, NKJV)

What about that perfect snapshot or video you thought you had of that memorable event? Then you took a look and realized it was out of focus or the video sound was not as clear as you thought. What was your reaction to the disappointment? A few reactions could be anger, regret, embarrassment, or even guilt. Stop and take a moment to breathe. For God is the Master of taking a broken heart, a tragic event, or the chaos when your best laid plans go wrong and using it to develop your character, increase your ability to hear His voice clearer, or even give you the ability to see His hand move on your behalf. When we veer off the path of destiny, God lovingly orchestrates events that will help us change our view and get back on track. The beauty of it is that God will use the challenging situations we experience to teach us to stay focused on Him.

A few days before my bridal shower, I had a discussion with my husband-to-be that could have derailed our upcoming nuptials.

God knows I was ready to call off the wedding. However, God used my family and friends who attended the bridal shower to encourage my heart. God changed my thoughts that night because He had a plan to bring two people who loved Him and would be His instruments for encouraging other couples. Marriage is not a fairy tale. It takes work, hard work, to make it to "death do us part" (and not wishing death on the other). God helps us to refocus our attention on things that will bring Him glory.

Prayer: Lord, thank You for the gentle way of reminding me to put my focus back on You when I have allowed life circumstances to blur my vision, my thoughts, and my path.

Day 13

REFOCUS: THOUGHTS AND PRAYER

_____
_____
_____
_____
_____
_____
_____
_____
_____
_____
_____
_____
_____
_____
_____
_____
_____
_____
_____
_____
_____
_____
_____
_____
_____
_____
_____

Day 14

RESILIENCE

:the ability of a substance to return to its usual shape after being bent, stretched, or pressed (dictionary.cambridge.org/us/, 2019)

"These things I have spoken to you, that in Me you may have peace. In the world you will have tribulation; but be of good cheer, I have overcome the world."

(JOHN 16:33, NKJV)

If you were training to run your first marathon, you could not simply sign up today and run tomorrow with any promise of a successful completion. You will need to first map out some sort of plan to help get your body into shape to endure the long run. It would be wise to discuss the plan with your physician prior to starting a training program. This will assist with knowing your limits. For beginner marathon runners, it is suggested that you embark on a year-long training program before even attempting any marathon. Training offers the runner the opportunity to learn their strengths and weaknesses. And it builds endurance.

I believe that the difficulties we face along our life's journey are used by God to strengthen our faith and our resilience. By enduring the smaller bumps and bruises, we build the ability to get back up when we are knocked on our butts. As strange as it may sound, seeing my mom deal with the daily pain of rheumatoid arthritis was my bumps and bruises experienced with her. Knowing that she had to deal with that pain was heart-wrenching for me. When my mother passed away, I held to the knowledge that she was finally free from that pain, and that helped me to live after her death.

It was difficult adjusting to a new normal as reality settled in that I would not physically talk to her every day. I was surprised that I did not go into full blown depression, and it was not because I did not want too. God had given me an emotional training program that prepared me to endure this new marathon.

Prayer: Lord, when You do the training, nothing can stop us. You give each of us the ability to bounce back after some extremely difficult situations (even the ones from which we are convinced that there is no coming back). Yet the best part, as we run this life race, You not only run with us but You have supporters along the route to give us water, and You are waiting for us at the finish line. I am so grateful that You have been with me from the start and will be with me until the end.

Day 14

Resilience: Thoughts and Prayer

_____
_____
_____
_____
_____
_____
_____
_____
_____
_____
_____
_____
_____
_____
_____
_____
_____
_____
_____
_____
_____
_____
_____

Day 15

REPLENISH

:to fill something again, or return something to its earlier condition (dictionary.cambridge.org/us/, 2019)

He will yet fill your mouth with laughing, And your lips with rejoicing.

(JOB 8:21, NKJV)

There have been moments of my life where I felt totally depleted in body, mind, and spirit, where darkness filled my thoughts and days. When you are in that space, it can be a challenge to even see the light let alone feel its warmth. At these very moments you have to remove the need to do it on your own. You won't be able to do it. You will need the love of God to help you through your valley. If you take a moment to stop and be still, you will see the flicker of light. The darkness will not overtake you.

While my mom was in the hospital, there were moments we shared when her humor prevailed over her pain. I recall one night as I was preparing to leave. I put my coat and hat on as I was saying, "Bye, I love you and will see you tomorrow." Then she stopped and looked at me and said, "You look cute."

She then proceeded to turn her head and look over by the chair near the window and the conversation went something like this:

"Don't my baby look cute?"

And I'm like, "Mom, who are you talking too?"

"That man over there?"

"What man, mom?"

"Don't you see that man sitting over there?"

"Mom, there is no man sitting there."

She smiled at me. I kissed her and told her I would see her tomorrow. As I was driving home, I began to cry and laugh thinking about what had just happened and the way she had just stopped to look at me and smile. It was this type of moment that helped me through another day seeing her bear the pain.

Prayer: For Isaiah 61:3 reminds me that You "console those who mourn in Zion, To give them beauty for ashes, The oil of joy for mourning, The garment of praise for the spirit of heaviness; That they may be called trees of righteousness, The planting of the Lord, that He may be glorified." Even when I am at my weakest point, I'm glad I can trust You, Lord, with those dark moments, and You will fill me with Your light again.

Day 15

REPLENISH: THOUGHTS AND PRAYER

_____

_____

_____

_____

_____

_____

_____

_____

_____

_____

_____

_____

_____

_____

_____

_____

_____

_____

_____

_____

_____

_____

_____

_____

_____

_____

_____

Day 16

REMARKABLE

:worthy of being or likely to be noticed especially as being uncommon or extraordinary (www. merriam-webster.com, 2019)

Saying with a loud voice: "Worthy is the Lamb who was slain to receive power and riches and wisdom, And strength and honor and glory and blessing!"

(REVELATION 5:12, NKJV)

When I think about the crazy things I have done in my life, I am thankful for the Lord's grace and mercy. You have to take a step back and really look at things in your life. It is noteworthy that the Lord has definitely seen me (and you) through the difficult times.

Each person handles life's difficult situations differently. For example, one couple may be able to work through infidelity whereas it is a deal breaker for another couple. One family can pull together during a death in the family yet another family will withdraw from each other. The remarkable part of it all is that we have a choice in how we work through each difficult situation. Is the hurt there? Most definitely! Yet God is able to carry you through when you make the choice to cast your burden upon Him. I've had to give my brokenness to the Lord many times. God is full of wonder, He has all power, and He is always worthy of our praise. His wonderful works are immeasurable.

Prayer: In You, Lord, I find power, glory, wisdom, blessings, and strength. Thank You for being a sacrifice so I may fully live. You are worthy of all praise!

Day 16

REMARKABLE THOUGHTS AND PRAYER

Day 17

RESOLUTE

:determined in character, action, or ideas
(dictionary.cambridge.org/us/, 2019)

Therefore, my beloved brethren, be steadfast, immovable, always abounding in the work of the Lord, knowing that your labor is not in vain in the Lord.

(1 CORINTHIANS 15:58, NKJV)

Your life's journey may feel chaotic at times. Your victories celebrated and your defeats can't be overlooked. Yet, through everything, you must settle in your heart that you are in it for the long haul. You have to be committed to that dream, goal, or purpose for each season of your life. It is very easy to stay dedicated to the cause when all is well or at least pretty good. But when the sugar honey iced tea hits the floor is when your character is revealed. Are you a warrior or a wimp? Although God fights the battle, are you one of His foot soldiers He can use as an instrument to shine for Him? Understand your mental capacity for dealing with life's challenges. When you have reached your maximum limit, look for that way of escape so you will be able to recuperate before you face the world again.

There it is… "again." You don't want to give up, you must try again. And again, and again. Be unwavering in your hope and surround yourself with the right people. They will be the ones who will keep you encouraged during your recovery yet push you to try again. Face it, you are more than a conqueror, and remember this when things are really tough and you are on the edge of a mental breakdown. Don't feel the need to go it alone. You are never alone.

I have had to stand firm on my faith and wait on the Lord to move me to my next career assignment. It has exhausted me spiritually and physically. Waiting has never been a favorite pastime. Especially when I know there is nothing impossible for God. But His mercy endures, and God has sprinkled nuggets along my path as a reminder that He is always with me, even when God seems to be silent. These nuggets come in the forms of family and friends whom I trust to talk things through, music that uplifts, or something I read that speaks to my situation. Be settled in your belief.

Prayer: Lord, although it has been a really tough season for me, I will praise You in all things. I will not waver from the reality that You are with me, always. Even if things do not change for me, I will stand firm in my commitment to God.

Day 17

RESOLUTE: THOUGHTS AND PRAYER

_____
_____
_____
_____
_____
_____
_____
_____
_____
_____
_____
_____
_____
_____
_____
_____
_____
_____
_____
_____
_____
_____
_____
_____
_____
_____

Day 18

RESONATE

:to produce or be filled with clear, continuing
sound (dictionary.cambridge.org/us/, 2019)

*Then Elijah said to Ahab, "Go up, eat and drink; for there
is the sound of abundance of rain." So Ahab went up to
eat and drink.*

(1 KINGS 18:41-42(A), NKJV)

The sound of rain. It can be a bit intimidating during a heavy storm, or the steady downpour can be a calming element when you simply sit and listen. In either situation, you can hear the sound of the rain. When you are experiencing a drought, you welcome the rain. You are looking for it to rain. You are praying for rain. The kind of rain you can hear because it is coming down hard.

For the past seven months, God has been pushing my hope and faith barometer. Notice that I said hope and faith. I have always felt my faith in God was strong. So much so that I did not realize doubt had invaded my heart and mind space. Although I was talking with God, I no longer was secure in my relationship with Him. My doubt was real. I did not recognize that God's hand was moving to fully restore my connection with Him. And to do that, He had to refill my hope to a place where it would reverberate deep down in my soul. Hebrews 11:1 states, "Now faith is the substance of things hoped for, the evidence of things not seen." The dictionary states that hope is a feeling of expectation and desire for a certain thing to happen. The meaning of faith is complete trust or confidence in someone or something. Complete trust in God's ability and not my own builds my understanding in the character of God (His sacrificial love, His forgiveness, and His praiseworthiness). Therefore, as my faith strengthens, it forces my emotions (my inner being) to believe with hopeful expectation that Jesus will see me through any circumstance.

Prayer: Lord, I am thankful for the things I have been fortunate enough to experience in my journey. I ask You to give me the faith to hope for those things that are yet to come. May my faith become such a sound that everyone in my path will hear (and see) it coming.

Day 18

RESONATE: THOUGHTS AND PRAYER

_____
_____
_____
_____
_____
_____
_____
_____
_____
_____
_____
_____
_____
_____
_____
_____
_____
_____
_____
_____
_____
_____
_____
_____
_____
_____

Day 19

REJUVENATE

:to make someone look or feel young and energetic again (dictionary.cambridge.org/us/, 2019)

But new wine must be put into new wineskins, and both are preserved. And no one, having drunk old wine, immediately desires new; for he says, 'The old is better.'

(LUKE 5:38-39, NKJV)

I have always wanted to visit a vineyard. Not necessarily for the taste-testing but to experience the beauty the vineyard displays. In the making of wine, a grape seed must first be planted. The seeds are nurtured until it is time to begin the steps for making the wine:

Step 1: the grapes are crushed.

Step 2: the grapes are fermented.

Step 3: the grapes are pressed to separate the wine from the grape skins.

Step 4: the wine is settled using large tanks.

Step 5: once the settling is done, the wine is put into small barrels for aging.

Step 6: when the barrel aging is completed, some wines are filtered to help stabilize and clarify them.

Step 7: finished wines are bottled.

And **Step 8:** there are some wines that are aged further in a bottle to deepen the taste of the wine.

In Luke 5:38, we are told not to pour new wine into old wineskins; new wine needs to be poured into new wineskins. Before the modern-day process of making wine explained in the above steps, wineskins were used to preserve the wine and flavor. New wineskins allow the grapes to expand during the fermentation process, which, in turn, stretches the wineskin. If you attempted to pour new wine into an old wineskin it would cause it to tear under the pressure of the new wine.

I see new wine as a metaphor for an opportunity to give new flavor in your life. Even through the difficult times, God will use every experience to bring new growth and awareness of your blessings. For a long time, it was hard for me to even talk about my mom without crying. I was not ready to lose her. Yet God brought to mind wonderful memories. It has given me a new outlook and a thankful heart that I have those memories. There is no way I would have been able to hold those memories in my anger about her death. He had to get me to a place where I was ready to be filled with those memories in a new way.

Prayer: Lord, thank You for giving me a new outlook on life after a tragic loss. I pray that I continue to look to You to fill the empty spaces of my life with new things, beauty, flavor, and joy.

Day 19

Rejuvenate: Thoughts and Prayer

_____
_____
_____
_____
_____
_____
_____
_____
_____
_____
_____
_____
_____
_____
_____
_____
_____
_____
_____
_____
_____
_____
_____

Day 20

REIGNITE

:to give new life or energy to (something) (www.
merriam-webster.com, 2019)

*Then the Lord answered me and said: "Write the vision
And make it plain on tablets, That he may run who reads
it.*

(HABAKKUK 2:2, NKJV)

*A*lthough it is difficult to do life after you deal with a
tragic event, you must choose the right path. You will
be faced with two options: allow depression, anger, or bitterness to
seep into your spirit or cast the heavy burden of hurt onto the Lord
so that your mourning will be turned into joy. Psalm 30:11 states,
"You have turned for me my mourning into dancing; You have
put off my sackcloth and clothed me with gladness." What I find
amazing in this process, is that the pain you have experience will
ultimately be used to encourage someone else along your journey.

You are God's vision, and when you surrender to Him, Jesus
will write His will on your heart. And when you let His love seep
into your heart and give Jesus your vulnerability, you will share it
in ways that will encourage others to get back in the game. Your
story will be the spark that will give light to another person's darkness, and that is all Jesus needs to reignite their purpose in their
life's journey.

The funny thing, God has used different people (family, friends,
and even strangers) to be that spark to keep me going. After I gave
birth to twins, I had a bout with post-partum depression. For the
first time, I understood the saying, "functional addict". After three

months of being home, I went back to work, did my wifely and motherly duties, but I was really depressed. I was in a black hole. My mother was the spark, and at moments, a torch that kept me going. But the one thing that stuck with me during the twins' early years is when she said, "Nikki, it will get better; remember every day they get a day older." She knew I was in a dark place even though I was smiling and laughing. She saw past my darkness and gave me hope I could run with.

Prayer: Lord, may I willingly be that spark that will help to encourage someone to keep running their race.

Day 20

REIGNITE: THOUGHTS AND PRAYER

_____
_____
_____
_____
_____
_____
_____
_____
_____
_____
_____
_____
_____
_____
_____
_____
_____
_____
_____
_____
_____
_____

Day 21

RE-ILLUMINE

Illumine: to put light in or on something
(dictionary.cambridge.org/us/, 2019)

*For You will light my lamp; The Lord my God will
enlighten my darkness.*

(PSALM 18:28, NKJV)

*For with You is the fountain of life; In Your light we see
light.*

(PSALM 36:9, NKJV)

I remember the day I was baptized at my Grandmother's
church. I can still clearly see me being dunked under the
water and then having a bright light shining on me through the
window. I felt like that light followed me to the back room of the
church where I dried off and changed back into my street clothes.
I was eleven years old. Yet when I was in my teens, I began having
suicidal thoughts, and for the life of me I'm not sure why (other
than the enemy trying to take me out early in the game). I felt
like I did not quite fit. Anywhere. I did not make friends easily,
and when I did it seemed that I was still on the outskirts of the
group. These emotions thrust me further into isolation. Yet there
was something deeper within my spirit that helped to subdue the
thoughts. Although I did not realize it back then, due to my im-
maturity, God was with me.

Prayerfully by now, you have come to realize that as dark as
your situation may be, or as deep as your tragedy may be, it will

not keep the love and light of Jesus from shining upon you. You have to trust God to see you through anything that life tries to throw your way. A good place to start is having hope to believe. Believe that God really does have a plan for your life. God even has a plan to use the hurt, the pain, the sadness, the despair to bless you and ultimately others who cross your path.

Through the trials of my life, I am still learning to regroup, rethink, or reposition during or after I face difficulty. This entails organizing my prayer and quiet moments with God (regroup), purposefully capturing my thoughts to keep them focused on Jesus (rethink), or consciously committing my ways to the Lord and placing my plans in His hands so my steps will be directed according to His plan (reposition). And the real success is being willing to do it again and again so you do not stay stuck during the tough moments.

Prayer: I am thankful, Lord, that I do not have to be afraid of the dark because You are always with me. You are my Light. My need for You has redeemed my time and sealed my eternity. My life will forever flow from Your love. In Jesus Name. Amen.

Day 21

Re-illumine: Thoughts and Prayer

_____
_____
_____
_____
_____
_____
_____
_____
_____
_____
_____
_____
_____
_____
_____
_____
_____
_____
_____
_____
_____
_____
_____
_____
_____
_____

Playlist (no particular order):

You Know My Name, Artist: Tasha Cobbs Leonard

Even If, Artist: MercyMe

My World Needs You, Artist: Kirk Franklin

You Are Not Alone, Artist: Psalm 23

~~You Say, Artist: Lauren Daigle~~

Cycles, Artist: Jonathan McReynolds

Surrounded (Fight My Battles), Artist: Michael W. Smith

Tell Me Where It Hurts, Artist: Fred Hammond

Acknowledgements

I want to thank my three children for reminding me, every chance they get, to laugh and enjoy life (and I will still remind them to stay focus).

I want to thank my entire family for the love you always showed my mother during her lifetime. And the continued love you show my Dad. God allowed my upbringing to shape me into the believer in Jesus Christ and woman I am today. I pray that God gives you each a bouquet of blessings.

Much Love & Blessings!

About The Author

Nikole Holt has been married to Rev. Milton Holt Sr. for 21 years. She is blessed to be a mom of three children and resides in Cheltenham, MD. Nikole has her Master's in Business Administration and has worked in the accounting field for over twenty-eight years. She enjoys sharing her love of Jesus Christ, listening to music and dancing (which brings her out of her natural introverted personality).

References

https://www.softchalk.com/lessonchallenge09/lesson/
wineTutorial/wineTutorial4.html, retrieved April 8, 2019.

Made in the USA
Middletown, DE
11 March 2022